EDUCATIONAL EQUALITY
AND THE NEW SELECTIVE
SCHOOLING

PREVIOUSLY PUBLISHED IN THE IMPACT SERIES

Impact
No.3

Educational Equality and the New Selective Schooling

BY HARRY BRIGHOUSE

Edited by John White

Published by the Philosophy of Education Society of Great Britain

First published in 2000 by the
Philosophy of Education Society of Great Britain

© Philosophy of Education Society of Great Britain

Distributed by Business and Medical Book Centre
9 Headlands Business Park
Ringwood, Hants BH24 3PB

British Library Cataloguing in Publication Data:
a catalogue record for this publication is available
from the British Library

ISBN 0 902227 04 1

Produced in Great Britain by
Reprographic Services
Institute of Education University of London

Printed by Formara Limited
16 The Candlemakers, Temple Farm Industrial
Estate, Southend on Sea, Essex SS2 5RX

P1/0002-IMPACT No3-01/2000

CONTENTS

THE IMPACT
EDITORIAL TEAM

Professor John White
(Editor)
Institute of Education
University of London

Professor Christopher Winch
(Deputy Editor)
Nene-University College
Northampton

Richard Smith,
University of Durham
Editor of the *Journal of
Philosophy of Education*

Dr Paul Standish
University of Dundee
Assistant Editor of the
*Journal of Philosophy
of Education*

Editorial introduction

This is the third pamphlet to appear in the IMPACT series, which is published by the Philosophy of Education Society of Great Britain (PESGB). Its purpose is to bring philosophical perspectives to bear on current British educational policy.

The response of policy-makers and the press to the first IMPACT paper – Andrew Davis's *Educational Assessment: a critique of current policy* , published in October 1999 – has reinforced our confidence that policy-makers and educationalists are interested in hearing philosophical explorations of key policy matters. In fact the response surpassed our expectations. Andrew Davis was invited to write complementary articles in the *Independent* and in the *Times Educational Supplement* . A symposium was held in November 1999 with Nick Tate of QCA, John Bangs from the NUT and Caroline Gipps of Kingston University. This

attracted participants from QCA, RSA, AEB, several LEAs, Head Teachers'
Review, Independent Schools Inspectorate, leading researchers in the
field of assessment, headteachers and academics. The print run of
IMPACT 1 is likely to be exhausted early in 2000.

Hence it has become clear to its sponsors within PESGB that its new
series is already beginning to have the effect on the policy-world which
its name reflects. With IMPACT papers appearing hard on each other's
heels it is too early at the time of writing (December 1999) to assess the
interest generated by our second pamphlet, but, given its topicality, it is
likely to be considerable. Michael Luntley's *Performance, Pay and
Professionals* is subtitled *Measuring the quality of teaching, a challenge to
the government's proposals on teachers' pay*. IMPACT 2 (publication date:
January 2000) is a no-holds-barred critique of the current government
proposals on performance-related pay for teachers. Among respondents
to Michael Luntley at a symposium on February 1 2000 are Nigel de
Gruchy of NASUWT, Sheila Lawlor of the think-tank Politeia and
Richard Pring of Oxford University.

Why have philosophers decided to enter the policy arena in this way?
I should say at once that this is not a wholly new initiative. For the last
three decades philosophers have both commented on policy and in some
cases contributed to its formulation. Their influence on official thinking
about the curriculum before and after the introduction of the National
Curriculum in 1988 is widely known. In addition they have been been
prominent in policy-related discussions of child-centred education, skills
and competences, privatisation, education in a multicultural society, the
rights of parents, school effectiveness, headteacher training, higher
education, spiritual and moral development, and many other topics.
Politically speaking, some have been on the left, some on the right, and
others unpigeonholable on either side.

Until now this work has been largely uncoordinated, the reflection
solely of individual interests. IMPACT is different. It is a collective venture
of the PESGB. It has arisen partly from awareness that the policy-focussed
work now regularly appearing in its *Journal of Philosophy of Education*

and elsewhere deserves a wider audience. Hence IMPACT 1 – which originated in Andrew Davis's 1998 JOPE monograph *The Limits of Educational Assessment* .

There has also been another motivation. Despite the intellectual vitality of the subject, the institutional base of philosophy of education has been massively eroded over the last twenty years. The number of teachers now aware of the philosophical dimensions of their work is tiny. Before the mid-1980s, in-service courses in philosophy of education were well-patronised. That was a time when central government always picked up the bill for students' fees. Since then, however, virtually every one of the few teachers who have studied the discipline has done so on private means.

One change in government policy which philosophers of education would like to see is greater encouragement – and this means more resources – for teachers to reflect on the values and assumptions underlying their work. The DfEE and QCA between them have worked hard since 1997 to create a National Curriculum for 2000 and beyond whose aims are spelt out far more fully than previously and whose detailed prescriptions are greatly reduced. These two reforms have been intended to complement each other. The idea has been that teachers who are more fully aware of why they are teaching what they are teaching can be given more flexibility in determining the routes to these broader goals. This presupposes reflective teachers who open-mindedly know their way around underlying aims and values, understand the interconnexions among them and are able to justify their own teaching activities in terms of them. All this requires a modicum of philosophical understanding.

Current government policy – both here and more specifically in its promotion of citizenship education – points to the need for greater institutional support for philosophy in teacher education. Indeed, without that support there is an increased danger of policy-makers and practitioners reinventing wheels, in virtual ignorance of work that has been done.

The Philosophy of Education Society of Great Britain has launched IMPACT not merely because it knows that the discipline has important bearings on educational policy. It also wants to bring this home to those who can make best use of these perspectives – policy-makers themselves. The text from Harry Brighouse in this volume is designed with precisely that purpose in mind.

Further IMPACT pamphlets are planned to appear late in 2000 and in 2001. The author of IMPACT 4, to be published in March 2000, is Christopher Winch, Professor of Philosophy of Education at Nene-College Northampton and deputy editor of IMPACT. His paper is entitled New Labour and the Future of Training. Within the framework of a discussion of the place of vocational aims among the aims of education in general, the pamphlet asks whether current post-16 training policy as put forward in the 1999 White paper *Learning to succeed* is likely to help deliver the government's stated target of a high skill economy.

Later topics for IMPACT pamphlets will include the new National Curriculum and its aims; citizenship education; good teaching; sex education; personal, social and health education; the place of modern languages in the curriculum; gifted pupils; environmental education. A full list will be found at the end of this pamphlet.

Each IMPACT paper expresses the ideas of its author only. It does not represent the view of the Philosophy of Education Society of Great Britain. There is indeed, no such single view. PESGB contains several hundred members whose ideas and political allegiances are widely disparate.

HARRY BRIGHOUSE is Associate Professor of Philosophy at the University of Wisconsin, Madison, in the USA. From September 2000, he will be Professor of Philosophy of Education at the Institute of Education, University of London. He works on political philosophy and philosophy of education, and has published articles in a wide variety of Philosophy and Education journals. He was led to his current interests in the political philosophy of education by his work on the foundations of liberalism, and his increasing dissatisfaction with the neglect, in recent liberal theories, of issues concerning children.

He is also a veteran political activist, having spent much of the last ten years working with a nascent left-wing political party in the U.S. called the New Party, and is on the steering committee of its Madison branch. He is a frequent contributor on education issues and British politics for the bi-monthly U.S.-based magazine, *Against the Current*. His recent book, *School Choice and Social Justice* (Oxford University Press, 2000) combines philosophical argument for a theory of social justice in education with an assessment of the empirical evidence concerning actual school choice schemes, and advocates a version of school choice which is designed to serve social justice.

Harry Brighouse's IMPACT pamphlet claims that the current policy of 'parental choice' of schools has introduced a *de facto* selective system at odds with the principle of educational equality. The first section of the paper presents a logically articulated case in favour of educational equality. The second draws on empirical evidence from a study by Gewirtz, Ball and Bowe to show how the policy of parental choice, as it has turned out in practice, compromises this equality. Section Three outlines what the author calls 'some modest egalitarian reforms' which could help to rectify the situation. These include the proposal that all schools should have a similar mix of class and ability levels; that resources are put into nursery education especially for low-income families; that wealth is redistributed from rich to poor; and that policy on children with special educational needs is revised. This section also includes responses to various objections – that there are no good reasons why schools should be heterogeneous in their composition; that the value of the family is being downplayed; and that Brighouse's proposals ignore the claims of educational excellence. There is also an insert on the private sector, which the author sees as a major source of educational and social inequality. He puts forward several practicable measures, again of a 'modest' sort, aimed at undermining this sector.

John White
January 2000

1
Introduction[1]

Since the 1970s the education system has been transformed by a series of radical reforms. The Conservative government's 1980 Education Act, taking its lead from a 1978 Labour government Bill, introduced a school admission system based on 'parental preference'. The 1988 Education Reform Act gave *substance* to the policy of preference by ensuring that data such as exam results would be published. This system has come to be called 'parental choice', but that name is misleading. As matters stand now parents' choices are not definitive: schools have a great deal of latitude over which children to admit. This supports the view, widespread among critics of the system, that selective schooling has been reintroduced under the guise of parental choice. This charge at least identifies the intentions of Kenneth Baker, the architect of the 1988 Act, who has said: 'I would have liked to bring back selection but I would have got into such controversy at an early stage that the other reforms would have been lost'. When asked if he understood that parental choice and the funding formula would kill off comprehensive schools, he replies, 'Oh yes. That was deliberate. In order to make changes, you have to come from several points.'[2]

The new de facto system of selection had dramatic effects in some areas. Nick Davies describes the effects of parental choice on two schools in Sheffield:

> There was a surge of anxiety about falling academic standards and a new wave of old-fashioned racial hostility. Abbeydale Grange suddenly found itself the scene of a full-blooded white flight ... the school which had once boasted 2,300 pupils had been abandoned by almost all of the white middle class and was left with fewer than 500 pupils. In the White Highlands, Silverdale was booming ... Middle class parents fled from Abbeydale Grange and bought their way into Silverdale's catchment area. No poor family from the north-east could afford to make the move ... poor children at Abbeydale Grange outnumbered the affluent by more than 3-1. Affluent children at Silverdale outnumbered the poor by the same factor ... Neither school is now comprehensive in anything but name.[3]

This is a stark example: but the pattern has been repeated more mutedly in most urban schooling 'markets': Baker's reforms have been remarkably successful by the standards he set himself.

While in opposition the Labour Party promised to abolish selective schooling. But in government it has moderated its stance. Those authorities which retain grammar schools, admittance to which is determined entirely by academic selection, must now allow parents in each schools catchment area to vote on whether to retain the grammar schools, as long as opponents can raise sufficient support in a petition process to trigger a vote. And the government has set up an Adjudicator's office to regulate local educational markets where some schools object to the admission practices of other schools: from its early performances it seems that this office will restrict academic selection to 20-30% of pupils in popular schools. Selection will, then, be mitigated, but it will remain in a substantial segment of most regional educational markets.

There are two distinct objections to selection. First is the comprehensive ideal. This applies directly to school populations, requiring that they be heterogeneous with respect to race, class background, and ability levels. Proponents of the comprehensive ideal think that schools should be composed so that future politicians, doctors, teachers, and business people should rub shoulders in their youth with future clerks, refuse-collectors, factory workers and secretaries. This stipulation is motivated partly by an anti-élitist principle – that those who will be privileged should be attuned to the interests of those who will be less privileged – but also partly by a more fundamental vision of the good society, which is one in which professional and income-status do not spill over into our judgments about civic status. Comprehensive schooling is expected to produce a more democratic ethos in which people regard each other as social equals despite material inequalities.

Second is the principle of educational equality – the idea that children have a right to an equal education regardless of their level of ability or social background.

Educational equality is a vague principle, and part of my aim in this pamphlet is to explicate it, in the light of the best argument, so a full explanation would be inappropriate at this stage. But I will note that proponents of educational equality have traditionally had at least two aims in mind, which any elaboration of the principle must take into account. First, they have aimed at ensuring that any child's prospects for educational achievement should be unaffected by the social class or educational backgound of his or her parents. Second, they have aimed at narrowing the gap in educational achievement between more and less academically talented children, by giving priority to devoting educational resources to the less talented. Educational egalitarians differ as to how much priority they attach to raising the educational achievement of the less talented, and a full theory of equality would provide a principle of priority. Unfortunately, while my argument does vindicate giving priority to the achievement of the less talented, it does not specify how much priority should be given, because I have not yet been able to answer that question satisfactorily.

While the comprehensive ideal is grounded in a picture of what the decent *society* would look like, the principle of educational equality focuses on what is owed to each individual. The comprehensive principle aims at social engineering, by indirectly influencing the social attitudes of the adults children will become; the principle of educational equality aims simply to equip those children with skills and abilities to enable them to negotiate the society they find themselves in, however that is organized. In contrast to the objection from the comprehensive ideal it is, at least, not obvious that selection violates educational equality: a case has to be made. It will turn out that educational equality does impugn selection as it has traditionally been practised in the UK though, as we shall see, selection of other sorts could, in principle, be educationally equal.

I shall ignore the comprehensive ideal here. My focus is entirely on the principle of educational equality and its consequences for selection. Defenders of selection usually argue that educational equality is not undermined by the reforms, or that educational equality is simply a less fundamental value than those of individual liberty and educational excellence. To confront these responses requires both philosophical argument, concerning the content of educational equality and its proper relationship to other values, and empirical evidence, concerning the operation of the new institutions. My argument has three main stages.

- In Section One I argue that educational equality is indeed, fundamental to a just society. Educational equality is much contested, both in philosophical and in public policy debates. My argument has the virtue of helping us to draw out some of the important normative features of educational equality as well as some of its practical consequences.

- In Section Two, drawing on studies of the operation of the post-1988 settlement, I shall identify the precise ways that educational equality is impeded.

- Finally, in Section Three, I shall propose a series of modest reforms that would move the system in the direction of equality. These reforms include:

  - Proposals to ensure that there every school has a similar mix of pupils in terms of both ability and social background.

  - Emphasis on the importance of putting extra resources into early schooling

- Streamlining of the process of statementing children with SENs.

- A series of reforms that would diminish the ability of the private sector to produce educational inequality

- Finally, and most controversially, I argue that educational equality requires reforms of the tax/benefit system aiming at greater equality of income and wealth. This, clearly, would not be a modest, but rather a radical move. I do not lay out a specific reform policy here, but merely emphasize a central implication of my argument: that educational equality cannot be seen as an alternative to traditional egalitarian goals, because it cannot be fully realized without those more traditional goals being realized first.

It is no part of my aim to defend a return to the system that preceded the 1980s. I know of no evidence that it was more successful at promoting educational equality than the current system. Even if such evidence existed it would not justify a return to it. As every teacher and administrator knows there are substantial transition costs associated with reform. The last thing the British educational system needs is another complete overhaul, and even if we could return to the past we could not be sure that it would work well now. The reforms I propose are deliberately modest – feasible reforms which can move us toward educational equality without imposing high transition costs.

2
Section One:
Why Educational Equality?

Some readers will find the concern with educational equality archaic. Political egalitarianism has suffered serious setbacks in recent years, and decreasing communication and transport costs combined with a system of world trade governance that supports capital mobility without enhancing labour mobility, has put increasing pressure on egalitarian policies.

The abandonment of egalitarianism in the face of these pressures is a serious error. There have been many successful attempts to limit the level of material inequality in capitalist societies, and many equalizing programmes, such as national health care systems, state pensions, child allowances, social security and unemployment support, are so widely supported that they are politically untouchable. We should not confuse the political pressure on egalitarianism with its undesirability. There are powerful reasons for continuing to struggle for egalitarian causes.

But the case for educational equality does not depend on the desirability of equality generally. The claim that people should be equally educated has no bearing on how much they should be paid after they leave full-time education. It states, instead, a condition on how they must be prepared for the quite possibly unequal material prospects which they will face in the world after the age of majority. In fact, my argument for educational equality *assumes* that material rewards in the labour markets will be significantly unequal, and takes that as one of the central reasons for making education equal. If anything, my argument suggests that the fact of material inequality – inequality of result – supports the case for educational equality, and then suggests that educational equality supports attempts to limit the extent of material inequalities.

One final preliminary. A just society will have a number of different aims in providing education. One of the aims, which is perhaps under-emphasized by policy makers but is inevitably close to the hearts of most educators, is to enrich the inner lives of children, by exposing them to the wisdom of the ages and facilitating their enjoyment of the fulfilment to be gleaned from the mastery and exercise of complex and demanding human skills. Another aim, which has gained increasing attention recently, is preparing children for effective participation in civic life.[4]

But I shall follow the general trend among makers of policy in focussing on two other aims: preparing children so that they can contribute to the general prosperity of the society they will enter, and preparing them so that they can benefit from the resultant prosperity: that is, equipping them with labour-market skills. Unlike the first, intrinsic, benefits, these latter benefits are to a significant degree, competitive in structure: education that improves the competitiveness of one child in the labour market will often thereby diminish the competitiveness of another child. I suspect that teaching the intrinsic benefits and the competitive benefits are so interlinked that aiming at equality in one will likely yield something close to equality in another, but my case here is entirely focussed on the competitive benefits.

The argument for educational equality is, initially, rather simple.

1. Where social institutions license unequal rewards, it is a *prima facie* requirement for their fairness that the competition for them is to ensure that the individuals who benefit from the rewards *deserve* to in some sense.

2. For inequalities of income to be fully deserved, educational inequalities must not be due to *i)* family background economic circumstances or *ii)* families' choices.[5]

Conclusion: Educational inequalities due to *i)* family background economic circumstances or *ii)* families' choices are *prima facie* unacceptable.

Is there any reason to accept both the premisses of this argument? Premiss 1 seems unobjectionable: it is part of the idea of fairness that people in some sense deserve their situation. The premiss does, however, depend on the idea that social institutions are constructs of human agency: institutions such as the market, for example, are not given parts of the natural order of things, but social constructs which we are able consciously to reform through public policy.

The premiss is furthermore, at odds with some traditions in recent political philosophy. Robert Nozick, in particular, claims that desert has no bearing on what we are entitled to, and that entitlement is the central notion in a theory of rights. John Rawls is often also interpreted as suggesting that desert has no role in a theory of justice, because he argues that there is no pre-institutional sense in which we deserve our holdings: we deserve whatever justice distributes to us: and justice, not desert, is the morally prior notion.

I do not have room here to refute Nozick's entitlement theory: it has been quite adequately dismissed elsewhere. But I am quite sympathetic with Rawls's rejection of a pre-institutional conception of desert. However, I would point out here that Rawls's defence of his theory of justice as fairness uses a notion that resembles closely the notion of desert I am appealing to here. His defence proceeds by means of a thought-experiment utilizing the so-called 'veil of ignorance': he asks what principles would be agreed to by hypothetical parties bargaining without knowing any of those facts about themselves which could be the grounds for some morally arbitrary bargaining advantage. But these features are precisely those which could not be the basis of desert, in the ordinary understanding of that notion on which my argument relies.[6] So despite my appeal to desert my argument should be seen as firmly within the Rawlsian tradition.

Premiss 2 might stand in more need of defence than premiss 1, but I think that defence is available:

a) Unequal rewards are only *deserved* to the extent that the candidates can reasonably be held fully responsible for their level of success in the competition for them.

b) If unequal inputs to a child's education are affected by i) family economic background circumstances and/or ii) his or her family's choices, labour market outcomes cannot reasonably be considered the full responsibility of the competitors.

Therefore 2. For inequalities of income to be fully deserved, educational inequalities must not be due to i) family background economic circumstances or ii) families' choices.

I take premiss a) to be relatively uncontroversial. There may be *other* reasons for thinking that people should, in some circumstances, keep benefits that they do not deserve, and the more weight we give to those reasons the more departures from educational equality we shall ultimately think can be licensed. But it is part of the idea of desert that people deserve what they are responsible for, and do not deserve what they are not responsible for. But what is the argument for premiss *b)*?

x) Where someone's level of success in the labour market is due *to some extent* to *i)* their family background economic circumstances or *ii)* his or her family's choices, it is unreasonable to hold the competitor responsible for *that level* of success to that extent.

y) Education significantly affects labour market outcomes – i.e. level of success in competition for higher levels of income – and the quality of educational inputs affects the quality of educational outputs.

Therefore *b)*. If unequal inputs to a child's education are affected by *i)* family background economic circumstances and/or *ii)* his or her family's choices, then labour market outcomes cannot reasonably be considered the full responsibility of the competitors.

Premiss *x)* seems reasonable. None of us is responsible for having been born to the parents we have, or for ending up in the adoptive family we ended up in. If that piece of fortune leads to benefits in the labour market, it is unreasonable to hold us responsible for having gained those benefits. Now, this is not to say that we are not responsible at all for our level of success in the labour market. On most accounts, the extent to which we exert effort in pursuit of some goal is something for which we can be held responsible, and even accounts which deny that will usually accept that it is proper to hold children responsible for the level of effort the exert because in doing so we are shaping the extent to which they will exert effort[7]. But the extent to which they can be held responsible cannot be isolated from the extent to which they cannot – we have no way of measuring exertion of effort independently of measuring achievement. So if, as desert seems to require, reward should be calibrated to features for which the individual can be held responsible, in practice labour markets will only be fair if the competitors in them have received educations which are equal in the sense described here.

Premiss *y)* is, I take it, a true empirical generalization. But it is worth noting that its truth is dependent on the economy being structured a certain way. We can imagine the economy being structured to reward only 'hours of work' ('to each according to their work'), or even so that education did not correlate with reward to labour (refuse-collectors get paid more than brain surgeons). It is widely believed that there are powerful reasons for wanting unequal rewards to labour: reasons to do with providing incentives for self-interested persons to be productive and the need to signal socially productive work even to altruistic agents. I shall not comment on these: I just assume the fact of inequality. No educator will want to deny the second part of *y)*: it is widely assumed in most industrial societies, but I should say that if it is false then most of the political and moral debates about schooling are robbed of their interest.

The argument for educational equality is, then, complete: and the principle of educational equality we can take from this argument is that educational inequalities due to *i)* family background economic circumstances or *ii)* families' choices are *prima facie* unacceptable.

Notice that the argument can only be a *prima facie* argument for educational equality. Desert is not the only value of justice, and the preservation of other values of justice may properly impede its full implementation, although as we shall see in section 3, much *can* be done consistent with the other values of justice.

But I should consider one immediate objection, which is that the conception of equal opportunity that underlies my argument is too strong. A weaker, and familiar, conception of equality of opportunity demands only that there be no arbitrary barriers in the way of people fulfilling their goals. So it requires careers open to talents, so that women or racial minorities, or people of low birth, may not be barred from pursuing any particular career path, but not that there be affirmative measures to assist the development of individuals born into less favourable circumstances. Before criticizing this alternative conception I should point out that I have carefully avoided using the term 'equal opportunity' in my argument: the content of the concept can ultimately be determined only by engaging in normative argument, so it is important to make the argument independent of the concept.

That said, the stronger conception of equal opportunity implicated in the basic argument is more true to the meanings of the words involved. Much of the rhetorical appeal of equal opportunity depends on the real meanings of the two terms involved. People who favour the weaker conception usually use the rhetoric of equality, and dispute the meaning of opportunity. But in fact the meaning of opportunity seems indisputable. Consider Florence and Dougal. Florence has £1000 to spend on a lottery, and Dougal has £1 to spend. Other things being equal, who has the greater opportunity to win? Again, Florence has £20,000 spent efficiently on her schooling; Dougal has £5,000 spent on his. Suppose that there are no arbitrary barriers to entrance, based on sex, class, ethnicity, religion, or other features. Who, other things being equal, has the greater opportunity to be admitted to Oxford University? We know who is more likely in both cases: it is Florence. To say that they have equal opportunity in either case is just false: Florence has more opportunity. Those who press this objection do not favour a different conception of equality of opportunity: they favour inequality of opportunity.

Now, a more sensible way of framing the objection would accept my characterisation of opportunity, and deny that it should be distributed equally. And in fact, I think there are reasons for objecting to particular measures that would be required to implement fully equal opportunity. But my argument establishes a strong presumption in favour of educational equality which can only be overcome by showing that other central values block measures that would be required for its implementation. In other words, the objection has force only if arguments can be produced to block particular measures. I shall consider these in the final section, when particular measures are proposed.

What exactly does educational equality mean? I indicated in the introduction that the concept is vague, and that making it more precise requires a normative argument for it of the kind I have given. I should warn the reader, again, that I do not have a full theory of educational equality. A partial account will suffice for the defence of the reforms in section 3, but a full philosophical account is still needed.

First, consider what educational equality means for two children, let's call them Julian and Sandy, who have the same level of talent, and the same willingness to exert effort to develop it. It requires, pretty clearly, that their educational prospects – the quality of schooling, likelihood that they will be qualified in their chosen areas, etc – be the same. In practice this means that equal resources should be spent on their educations.

Of course, if Julian comes from a wealthy family that values education, while Sandy comes from a poor family that despises education, equal spending on them in school will not yield educational equality, since Julian gets extra education elsewhere. Fully implementing educational equality between them will require the state to do more for Sandy than for Julian, and this justifies, at the very least, powerful state support for nursery education of poor children, and increased funding for primary schools in low-income catchment areas. Fully equalising education between Julian and Sandy, however, would require the state to know a great deal about both families, to place limits on Julian's family, and, perhaps, to exhort Sandy's family to alter their values. The limits would be unacceptably intrusive – it is crucial to the health of family relationships that parents be free to share their enthusiasms with their children – and many people would be wary of having the state trying to engineer the values of parents. So the government will be restricted to two kinds of measure: enriched schooling for poor children, and limiting the inequalities of income and wealth that support many of Julian's advantages.

The policy implications of educational equality between children of the same level of ability seems straightforward: the government must attempt, as far as is possible while respecting other central values, to eliminate the effects of social class on achievement.

But the implications are much less clear with respect to inequalities of ability. Return to the argument for educational equality and substitute 'level of natural talent' for 'family circumstances or choices' and you will find that the argument appears just as powerful. Its new conclusion, though, is that 'educational inequalities due to inequalities of level of natural talent' are *prima facie* unacceptable. In the case of social class educational inequalities are most naturally understood in as inequalities of outcomes. But to impugn inequalities of outcome between, for example, a child with severe cognitive disabilities, and a motivated child with a 120 IQ would seem absurd: attaining equal outcomes would require that we completely neglect, or even disable, the child with the 120 IQ.

However, there is a consensus on the idea that children with identifiable disabilities, or with Special Educational Needs, should have more money spent on their educations than those without, although the consensus does not support the absolute priority suggested by the argument for educational equality. If the justification of that consensus is that children with special educational needs need to have additional resources in order to get a full education, I see no reason why the same should not apply to children who, though not disabled, have less natural talent than others. The argument suggests, then, that, other things being equal, more resources should be devoted to less talented than to more talented children. This is a vague injunction, but it may not be so hard to operationalise. In practice talent is hard to measure, because it is impossible to disentangle from achievement, its observable consequence. In addition children are resources for each other. So the practical consequences of the injunction may be that schools should seek entering student bodies that are heterogenous with regard to achievement, and then prioritise raising the lower achievement levels.

I shall refrain from pressing the claim that more resources should be spent on less talented students because, beyond what I have just said, I do not have a principled guide to how many more resources they should have. I shall use instead the more urgent principle that at least equal resources should be spent on less talented as on more talented students.

3
Section Two:
How Schooling Compromises Equality

How does parental choice lead to selection and compromise educational equality? Answering this question is vital for the defence of reforms I shall offer: especially the requirement that school populations be heterogeneous and the streamlining of the process of statementing children with SENs. These reforms are responses to particular mechanisms that impede educational equality, which mechanisms have to be revealed by study of the system. In uncovering these I shall rely heavily on the study by Sharon Gewirtz, Stephen J. Ball and Richard Bowe entitled *Markets, Choice and Equity in Education*.[8] Gewirtz et. al. looked at the operation of the 1988 reforms in three overlapping local education markets in London. Their research looked at both the demand side – how parents chose schools – and the supply side – how schools attracted and selected pupils. Their data consisted of interviews of parents, interviews of administrators, governors, and teachers in the schools, interviews of administrators at the LEAs involved, and various materials pertaining to school enrolment, choices, school performance indicators, and LEA planning meetings.

There are two problems with drawing firm conclusions from the Gewirtz et. al. study. First, the data was collected from 1991-1994, some time after the reforms had been introduced, but before the effects of the reforms were in any way settled. Secondly they have not gathered the fine-grained data which would most help us to make confident conclusions about equality. From this perspective the ideal study would be quantitative, and would demonstrate either an improvement or decline in achievement for the least able and poorest pupils relative to the most able and wealthiest children, and show the change to be stable.[9] So any conclusions must be somewhat tentative.

What were their findings?

The Demand Side

On the demand side they found a distinct difference, correlating strongly with the social class and educational background, in the ways parents choose. They distinguish three classes of chooser.

- 'Privileged, or skilled' choosers , mostly better educated parents, are better able to understand the public sources of information, including the information offered by the schools themselves. They display 'a marked scepticism about the attempts at impression management involved in the production of school prospectuses and in the organization and choreographing of open evenings and school tours'.[10] They are much more likely to take control of the process of choice, and less likely to allow their children to make the choice themselves. They also display a consistent concern with the social origins of the likely peer group, and an interest in having the child among bright children.

- Semi-skilled choosers are less aware than the skilled choosers of the need to find a good match between the school and their child: as Gewirtz et. al. put it, 'the process of school choice is abstract, more a matter of finding the 'good' school rather than the 'right' one'.[11]

- Finally the least well-educated or 'disconnected' choosers, 'almost always began with, and limited themselves to, two [schools]. These would be schools in close physical proximity and part of their social community [whereas the skilled choosers tended to arrive at two schools after a winnowing process]'.[12] The disconnected choosers do not talk about child personality or teaching methods, but focus on 'factors such as facilities, distance, safety, convenience, and locality'.[13]

Gewirtz et. al. conclude that the unequal sophistication of parents as choosers in the educational marketplace bodes ill for educational equality. Prima facie we would expect that the worse choosers would get worse schools for their children, and that the privileged children of privileged choosers will tend to congregate together in schools where they can transmit advantages to one another. It should be easier to teach them than the children of the less skilled choosers, and if school budgets are responsive almost exclusively to the age and number of pupils in the school we would expect the per-pupil allocation of effective educational resources to be greater in the schools with more privileged pupils.

The Supply Side

Of course, these expectations of inequality could be confounded by unexpected behaviour on the supply side. If, for example, schools all sought a mix of socio-economic class and of ability levels within the school body, they would be likely to differentiate their kinds of outreach so as to attract all kinds of chooser, and would adjust their admissions policies similarly.

However, as Gewirtz et. al. find, the supply side has also responded to the reforms in a way that would lead us to expect inequality. Some school management teams embraced the need to market their school with enthusiasm, others embracing it as a necessary evil in the light of the changed environment. But the incentives are clear, and schools are all pursuing, to a greater or lesser degree, the more desirable pupil base: pupils who are identified as able, well-motivated and middle class, and especially girls and children with South Asian backgrounds. These are the pupils viewed most likely to improve the test scores which will serve as the performance indicators which will be used to attract further desirable applicants in the future. Even management teams deeply committed to some sort of comprehensive ideal are forced by the logic of the market conditions they face and the content of their ideal into this sort of marketing: a comprehensive school without able pupils and middle class pupils is not a comprehensive school, but a lower-tier school in a selective system.

The behaviour on the demand and supply sides interact to produce inequality: when schools have discretion over admissions and are not rewarded materially for admitting pupils who are difficult to teach, they will naturally aim for the more easily teachable pupils; and if the parents of the more easily teachable pupils are able to identify the best schools for their children we can expect inequalities to emerge.

Compromising Equality

That schools aim at the more easily teachable pupils leads to two distinct kinds of cleavage, each of which compromises educational equality. First, children from wealthier and better educated homes tend to concentrate in particular schools while children from lower-income and less well educated homes concentrate in others. There is, in other words, a tendency to class segregation. Second, though, higher-achieving and lower-achieving children are increasingly segregated, as under the grammar school system. Popular schools are able to fill their places from the preferred groups. These schools then need fewer resources than others because the children are less expensive to teach. The sting in the tail is that the funding formula ensures that these schools have even more effective resources per pupil than the schools which need more. A school's funding is keyed to the number of pupils it attracts, so that each child brings with it a fixed marginal sum. Fixed costs are a much greater part of the school's costs than is recognised by the funding formula. So a popular school's marginal income will exceed its marginal costs, allowing it extra effective resources to spend on its already advantaged pupils. But an unpopular school's fixed and marginal costs might well exceed its total income, so that resources must be diverted to the running costs of the school.

The consequence of this for the distribution of effective educational resources should be obvious. The popular schools, which have pupils with fewer needs have, other things being equal, more effective resources per pupil than less popular schools. Any amount of selection allows popular schools to claim the more able and socially advantaged pupils; and thus violates the minimal demands of educational equality. Less popular schools cannot even promise smaller classes, since the budgeting requires teachers to be redeployed away from them.

Another factor worsens the situation with regard to ability. Schools have considerable discretion over whether to admit children with special educational needs (SEN) who are, by definition, more expensive to educate. Yet the extra funds which follow children with SEN do not usually cover the additional costs of educating them. Schools aiming to do well by pupils with special needs face the following dilemma, nicely summarized by one of Gewirtz. et. al.'s interviewees (a school governor):

> The school has an enormous intake of SEN (special education needs) ... But that's another thing; you work hard, you develop an area, you get known as a good school for SEN and so what happens? – you're flooded with SEN kids which don't drag the resources with them that they need and so disproportionately affect the resourcing of the school.[14]

If parents believe (as Gewirtz et. al. claim that many do) that schools which contain disproportionate numbers of children with disabilities cannot educate academically more able children well, and if, as is the case, children with special needs do not bring with them all the resources that will have to be devoted to them in the school, schools face a disincentive to provide well for those pupils. The prejudice is exacerbated by the manner of publication of exam results: schools are required to publish raw scores in school leaving examinations, without reference to entry-level scores, so that children with special needs pull down the 'grades' by which the school will be evaluated.[15] In keeping with these incentives, the study found that 'it is provision in those schools which have the greatest numbers of children *requiring* learning support which is most vulnerable because such schools tend to be the ones which are undersubscribed and so financially less secure' and that teachers were routinely redeployed away from special needs departments even as numbers of pupils with special needs increased.[16]

4
Section Three:
Some Modest Egalitarian Reforms

Before outlining and defending the egalitarian reforms, I should explain exactly what conclusions can be drawn from the Gewirtz et al findings. We can conclude that there is an equality deficit in the new system: in particular that its children who are socially or intellectually disadvantaged or whose parents are poor choosers can be expected to have fewer effective educational resources devoted to them for those reasons. We cannot, however, conclude that the framework of the 1988 Reform Act is inferior to the one it replaced, with respect to equality, for three reasons.

● First, there is no evidence concerning the efficiency effects of the reforms: if, as the proponents of choice argue, efficiency is enhanced, the improved educational benefits for the least advantaged pupils may compensate somewhat for the expected inequalities.

- Second, it may be that the differentiation of the parents as choosers is an artifice of the newness of the reforms. It would not be surprising if the privileged choosers easily accommodated to the new system, but it also would not be surprising if the disconnected choosers should become more sophisticated over time. Effective choosing is a skill that can, to some extent, be learned.

- Finally, and most importantly, the Gewirtz study is not a comparative study between the egalitarianism of the new system and that of the old. The researchers quote Kenneth Clarke's ironic comment that when the comprehensive schools replaced academically selective schools in the 1960's 'selection by mortgage replaced selection by examination and the eleven-plus route was closed for many bright working-class boys and girls'.[17] In the pre-1988 arrangements, even without *de jure* choice, there was *de facto* choice: wealthier parents could purchase houses in the catchment areas of desired state schools, opt for the private sector, or use their talents at working the system to have their children accepted to their preferred school. Those most advantaged by the new reformed system are precisely the same people who could take best advantage of the previous system.

We need reforms that will move us toward educational equality without demoralising teachers and with minimal disruption of administration. The study cited identifies two obvious and avoidable sources of educational inequality: the unequal choice-making ability of parents; and the fact that fewer resources follow children with SEN to schools than are needed to educate them. There are at least two other equally serious sources of inequality.

First, inequality of income and wealth is a major source of educational inequality. Children from better-off homes have access to a range of educational experiences outside school that are not available to others, and these benefits inevitably spill over into the classroom. They can converse with better-educated adults, they have access to tutors, to music lessons, to foreign holidays, etc. They can afford a more relaxed attitude to financial risk, and, knowing that they can forgo earnings in young adulthood, they can aspire to university attendance, thus making their current achievement in school more significant to them. Educational equality is unavoidably compromised by inequality of household wealth as long as we allow parents to raise their own children.

Second, of course, in the UK the private sector selects children by a complex of wealth, status and income: the main function of the private sector in the UK is to ensure that successful parents can transmit their social advantages to their children through education (see insert below).

The Private Sector

The operation of the private sector is probably the single greatest institutional source of educational inequality, as well as of social inequality. Wealthy parents are able to, and do, send their children to schools which have available to them fantastic resources, and in from which children who are educationally or socially disadvantaged are largely absent, and in which no-one is *both* educationally and socially disadvantaged. The argument against private schooling is familiar: when wealthy parents can remove their children from the state sector, the state sector is deprived of such children but also of the support and involvement of their parents. A popular view is that the *Universal Declaration of Human Rights* and the *European Convention of*

Human Rights include provisions that make it illegal to prohibit private schools. The relevant provisions, however, assert quite implausibly strong parental rights over education, and the documents are therefore flawed. However, it is clear that prohibition is not on the political agenda in the foreseeable future. So educational egalitarians are cornered: they must either be silent about private schools, or advance measures short of prohibition that will make the private sector less popular.

I will suggest a series of modest measures that would help to undermine the private sector, all of which can be justified on independent grounds.

1. Private schools could be prohibited from selecting on the basis of ability. This may seem bizarre: it would make parental wealth an even more significant determinant of access to élite private education than it now is. But, in doing so, it would make private schools less attractive to parents with bright children: it would compromise the product to some extent.

2. Private schools should be required to publish value-added exam results, and the DFEE should publish a comparison between each individual private school and comparable state schools. Since most private schools owe their success to their intake, this would make private schools less attractive by demonstrating the superiority of comparable state schools in value-added terms. It can be defended, however, on the grounds that it makes information more transparent and therefore assists the working of the market within the private sector.

3. Funding for state schools should be increased across the board, which increases should go exclusively to affecting those remediable factors which cause parents to opt into the private sector (class size, special academic programmes, etc.). All well-managed increases in spending in the state sector increase its attractiveness relative to the private sector, because they improve the state sector, which is justifiable on independent grounds.

4. Charitable status should be withdrawn from private schools. This measure is consistent with market ideology, and would enable for-profit private schools to enter the private sector on a more equitable basis. It would also drive up the costs of private schooling, to the advantage of the state sector.

These measures are, as I say, modest, and would not undermine the private sector. But they would level the playing field somewhat, and would diminish the problem faced by the state sector when it competes for children with wealthy parents who have cultural capital and political influence. I should emphasize the contingencies that lead me to support these measures. Were private schools more central to the ordinary operation of educational markets, as they are in the United States, I might support measures that strengthen them (and I do support some such measures in the U.S.). But in the U.K. their major role is to draw children who are already privileged away from the state sector, and confer on them additional privileges, and there is no prospect of their playing a different role. In these circumstances the proper egalitarian strategy is to design policies like these, which can weaken the sector consistent with the (flawed) human rights documents that constrain national legislation.

No single government, even with a massive majority, can expect to overcome all these sources of educational inequality. I am about to recommend a series of reforms that would clearly move the system toward the ideal of educational equality. I believe that these reforms are, for the most part, modest: while they may make great demands on the public purse, they do not require a massive overhaul of the institutional framework of education provision. They are, in that sense, extremely modest when compared with the introduction of the quasi market and the National Curriculum in the 1980's. They are, that is, relatively conservative reforms.

This is not to deny that these reforms face serious barriers. But these barriers are *political*, not institutional. The reforms would not produce perverse effects, and would be institutionally self-sustaining over time. They appear ambitious not because of their internal structure, but because the principle underlying them, educational equality, is not favoured by the people who shape public debate about education, and because there is an understandable popular scepticism about equalizing measures generally. But neither the public stance toward egalitarian reform nor the chattering classes' attitudes toward educational equality are unchangeable data. The duty of intellectuals is to make the best arguments they can for principled stances in politics, and to offer creative and plausible proposals for reform. These arguments and proposals can and sometimes do affect what people believe, and hence what is politically possible. I take this to be what Erik Wright has in mind when he says that 'nurturing clear-sighted understandings of what it would take to create social institutions free of oppression is part of creating a political will for radical social changes to reduce oppression'.[18]

Here, then, are the proposals:

1. The Heterogeneity Requirement:

A crucial step toward educational equality would be to try to ensure that every school has a similar mix of class and ability level among its students. There are two ways of trying to achieve this. The first is to provide substantial financial incentives to schools to achieve the prescribed mix, tailoring the marginal per-pupil amount provided to the schools to the prior mix of pupils. For example, if a school has a higher than prescribed mix of high ability children it would receive no extra funds for its next high-ability pupil, but would receive twice the normal funds for admitting a low ability pupil. This method has a great deal to recommend it in a more market-based system than in the UK. Its disadvantage is that in order to be effective it must penalize schools that contain a concentration of low-ability or working class students, thus worsening the problem of educational equality in the short to medium term.

The other method is to require schools to select from among their applicants by a lottery. Geoffrey Walford has already advocated the use of lotteries. Their use is not novel: in the Milwaukee Public Choice Program in the United States, in which the State provides vouchers for children from low-income families to attend private schools, oversubscribed participating schools are required to select by lottery. But lotteries in the U.K. system can be expected to have at least one bad effect: increased targeting of advertising, to try and increase the proportion of 'desired' pupils in the applicant pool. For this reason I suspect that a mix of the two methods will be necessary to achieve the desired result.

2. Early Schooling:

Educational equality directs our attention most urgently to the early years. A government committed to educational equality will attempt to dramatically extend the provision of nursery education, especially to children from low-income families, and this is the single area of policy where the 1997 Labour government has excelled. This is, of course, costly, especially because teacher-pupil ratios must be very high. But where justice demands something, it has a very high priority: the costs must be paid, unless doing so jeopardises some other provision of justice. Educational provision in the early years, furthermore, is one area of social policy where means-testing makes sense, so it is reasonable to require that parents with higher incomes pay more for provision[19]. However, it also makes sense to attempt to achieve class and ability mixing, so that high-income families would receive a significant subsidy for sending their children to nursery schools with low-income pupils, but not for sending them to schools with other middle-high income pupils.

3. Level Wealth:

The Labour government elected in 1997 has made genuine, good faith, efforts to improve educational equality within the system. But it has not attempted seriously to mitigate background inequalities of income and wealth. Yet the slogan 'Education, Education, Education' implies that schooling cannot be the sole focus of education policy, for so much education happens outside schools, and in the home. Anyone who believes, as I do, both in the importance of the family and the principle of educational equality must object to substantial inequalities of household income and wealth, for they are the enemies of educational equality.

The above statement requires explanation. I believe that the family is the most suitable arrangement available for the rearing of children, and for that reason believe that it must be supported by social arrangements, and that children should grow up within their families, and parents should have a great deal of discretion over their childrens' upbringings. But such discretion allows parents to confer upon their children extensive educational benefits outside schooltime: they can teach them to read, pay for private tuition, take them on educationally valuable holidays, etc. Children growing up in financially secure homes have additional advantages: more space, freedom from the need to work during their school years, and (some) freedom from the stresses on the family that inevitably accompany poverty. If we care about educational equality, or equality of opportunity, but also believe that children should be reared by their parents, we are bound to look dimly on substantial inequalities of household income and wealth, because such inequalities predictably cause inequalities in education and opportunity.

A government serious about educational equality must defy the current political consensus and aim to redistribute wealth. Educational egalitarians should welcome substantial redistribution from rich to poor, as long as the mechanisms involved are well-designed. There is not scope here to defend any particular proposal, only to emphasize that educational equality requires strict limits on material inequality.

4. Students with SEN:

The key problems with students with SEN, which has a knock-on effect on other students, seem to be that the funds following students with SEN are insufficient, and that the process of statementing is controlled by the Local Education Authority (LEA) which is also the funding source. Although parents can appeal a statementing decision to a tribunal, schools cannot, and the content of the appeal is limited. I would suggest a reassessment of the funding of statements, and the establishment of an independent statementing body, which is not accountable to the LEA. This will, of course, tend to raise costs, but an additional measure could help lower them. The government could introduce incentives for schools to specialise in the education of children with particular kinds of SEN, gaining potential economies of scale.

I anticipate resistance to all of these proposals, but most

particularly to the heterogeneity requirement and to the injunction to level wealth. So before concluding I want to discuss some objections to those elements.

A. Objections to the heterogeneity requirement

Two objections to the heterogeneity requirement immediately present themselves, one on the supply side, the other on the demand side. A common argument against this kind of regulation of schools is that it prevents schools from differentiating themselves adequately. Part of the product of a school is the composition of the school itself, and if management teams have no effective power over composition they also lack power, to that extent, over the design of the product. The effectiveness of school choice in promoting good practices and high attainment overall depends on the ability of schools to differentiate their product. *The Economist* lauds the former Conservative government because it 'recognised that the best way to make schools effective is to give them a distinctive ethos ... Allowing schools to establish their own character means giving them more influence over which pupils they admit'.[20] Selection, then, is essential to allowing schools to develop their own characters which is, in turn, valuable both for allowing the market to operate efficiently and to making schools effective.

This objection must be resisted. Schools can differentiate their product in other ways than by determining admissions: they can vary their course offerings, specialise in the arts or sciences, choose whether or not to require uniforms, establish links with other schools, etc. One way they should not be allowed to differentiate, if we are committed to educational equality, is by offering more effective resources to more able pupils. The benefits of 'distinctiveness' can be gained without compromising equality. Furthermore, the heterogeneity requirement helps mitigate an unavoidable market imperfection. In neoclassical economic theory the efficiency benefits of perfect markets depend on the idea that firms are price takers, meaning that they have no control over the market price of their product and cannot select their customers.

But in real educational markets this is impossible. To survive schools must be over a certain size, and this limits the number of schools in any regional market. That limitation means that in any regional educational market there will never be enough schools for anything approaching perfect competition: it creates a serious and irremovable market imperfection.[21] Administrative costs and the importance to parents of not disrupting their children's schooling mean that supply will not adjust to demand rapidly, let alone instantaneously. In fact, there is a case for regulation on the demand side to limit the number of times parents could switch schools, both to prevent disruption and to pressure parents to take their choices very seriously. So schools, unlike firms in a perfect market, will have a great deal of power over consumers. The heterogeneity requirement, like any other requirement that effectively deprives schools of power over their composition, returns market power to the parents which they otherwise would not have. It makes the market more perfect.[22]

On the demand side a quite different objection rears its head, appealing to the principle of freedom of association. Parents should be free to have their children associate with others whom they have chosen. Heterogeneity requirements deprive them of that freedom: it is impossible for parents to determine which other children their children will associate with. I want my child to associate with atheists, my next door neighbour wants hers to associate with Christians, and the man next to her wants his children to associate mainly with clever kids. Unless schools can differentiate themselves on these sorts of basis, parents are deprived of this sort of freedom.

Again, this objection must be resisted on two grounds. First, to the extent to which they control selection, schools *deprive* parents of freedom to determine with whom their children associate anyway.

Your child does not attend the school you have chosen: she attends the school that has chosen her. When Danny Joscelyne, who has Down's Syndrome, was rejected by the mainstream secondary school into which most of his primary schoolmates were admitted, his parents were prevented from exercising freedom of association on his behalf.[23] Either freedom of association is a right, in which case all have it guaranteed and schools are deprived of all power over admissions, or it is not a right, in which case its invocation does not constitute an objection to strict regulation of admissions.

The second reason to reject this objection is simply that parents do not have an absolute right to determine with whom their children should associate. The right to freedom of association is an important right, but it is so because choosing with whom we associate is central to our ability to govern the course of our own lives. Children are not adults in miniature: they are potential adults, who need to learn how to become self-governing. As such they do not have a right to freedom of association themselves, but neither do their parents have absolute freedom to determine with whom they may associate.

The above are objections of principle. But there are also more pragmatic objections to the heterogeneity requirement. In the major cities achieving heterogeneity in schools would require that children be bussed around the city, since neighbourhoods tend to be class segregated. In some rural areas it may simply be impossible to achieve heterogeneity even with bussing, since the catchment areas may be impracticably large. I suggest that the DfEE, which would be charged with overseeing this requirement, should be allowed to give waivers from the requirement to schools in sparsely populated areas. But the necessity for increased travel expenses in urban and suburban areas troubles me less. Travel expenses are made necessary by two things: parental choice and class-segregated housing. The heterogeneity requirement would create a long-term incentive for city planners to integrate housing, which would be a good thing in itself. But more importantly, if the market in schools is going to produce efficiency benefits, parents should not face unequal barriers to making their choices. One of the reasons Gewirtz et. al.'s disconnected choosers seek the closest school is that the opportunity costs of sending their children to a distant school are much higher for them than for the skilled choosers. Parents must bear the costs and inconveniences of sending their children to distant schools, which costs comprise a much greater proportion of disposable income for poor than for wealthy parents. They therefore constitute a greater barrier to those parents, and a serious inequality and market imperfection. Increased travel costs to the LEA are a prerequisite of making the market in schools more efficient.

B. The Value of the Family Objection

It is commonplace to draw a distinction between two distinct goals: equality of opportunity and equality of outcome. Equality of outcome is often derided as a discredited goal, while equality of opportunity is lauded as admirable and achievable. But as I have already explained, as long as children are raised in families, inequality of outcome is a serious barrier to equality of opportunity: in the real world the two principles describe complementary, not contrary, goals. However, levelling wealth, and inhibiting private schooling, in service of educational equality are sometimes criticized for undermining the value of the family. It is part of the value of the family, on this view, that parents can transmit their values and advantages to their children.

The family is, indeed, a central moral institution and egalitarians do and must keep this in mind when proposing reforms. But we could not conclude from the centrality of the family that, for example, it should be permissible for parents to buy their children places at Oxford or Cambridge Universities, or that they be allowed to pay juries to acquit their accused children. It is uncontroversial that justice imposes limits on what parents may do for their children. The central concern with the value of the family is that institutional proposals must not unduly limit the ability of parents and children spontaneously to share each other's enthusiasms, or inhibit the intimacy from which children (and parents) learn so much.

But none of the above proposals does, or threatens to do, that. All the proposals limits the ability of parents to use *resources other than themselves* to confer advantages on their children. Even levelling wealth does not threaten the family: formerly wealthy parents will have less money to spend on their children, but they will have no less of themselves to share with their children. In fact, since poverty is a major factor in disrupting the smooth operation of the family, levelling wealth can be expected to benefit the institution.

It might be responded that when parents claim the right to determine the content and provision of their children's educations, what they care about is not their relationships with their children, but that they be able to shape the value and life prospects of their children. Of course, for some parents this is true (though for fewer, I suspect, than many philosophers have thought). But it doesn't follow from the fact that someone desires something, however intensely, that they have a *right* to it. Of course, the measures I propose limit what parents can do to shape the life prospects of their children. But this in itself cannot be an objection. Making education compulsory to age 16 limits the ability of parents to shape the life prospects of their children because it prevents some from depriving their children of education, but also reduces the labour market chances of other children by increasing the pool of potential competitors. Imposing the national curriculum on state schools means that parents who wish their children not to learn the prescribed skills cannot have what they want. Any theory which gives parents the extensive rights over their children suggested by this objection fails to respect the separate moral standing of the child, whose future is in trust to both the parent and the state, but whose future is fundamentally his or her own.

C. The Educational Excellence Objection.[24]

After the government introduced its scheme for allowing parents to petition for the abolition of grammar schools in those areas where they still exist, Eric Hammond, a former Trade Union leader, objected that the government seems to think that all children should be treated the same, whereas in fact brighter children deserve and need a different kind of education. Excellence is often cited as a reason for selection: contrary to the recommendations of educational equality, bright children must be selected out and given special nurturing so that they can scale the intellectual heights.

Any intellectual who dismisses concerns with excellence is being disingenuous, and I cannot say that the excellence objection does not worry me. But the excellence objection is very unclear as it stands. There are three broad kinds of motivation for this objection.

- The idea that excellence is desirable for its own sake

- The idea that more able children deserve more resources to be spent on their education

- The idea that there is a social benefit, accruing to all of society, to distributing education so that brighter children achieve more than less bright children.

- The excellence for its own sake position is suggested by several conservative writers about education. John Wilson suggests it when he argues that society should 'allocate [educational] resources to those who can best profit from them.'[25] David Cooper draws similar distributive conclusions from the fact that there is 'a fundamental human concern with the attainment, in whatever field, of excellence; the concern that some should scale the heights.'[26] He compares excellence in education with that in athletics and music: 'the prime concern of the lover of music or athletics is not with a general, marginal improvement in the amateur playing of string quartets, or in the times clocked by run-of-the-mill club runners; but with seeing the highest standards of musicianship maintained and advanced, with seeing great athletes break new barriers.'[27] He goes on to associate himself with the tradition 'of those who see a prime value of education to consist in the transmission and fostering of (certain kinds of) understanding, knowledge, critical appreciation and the like for their own sake.'[28]

Justice is concerned with the distribution of goods to people, and is interested in the generation of goods only in so far as those goods can be enjoyed by people. Wilson makes the mistake of treating justice as if it is about distributing people to goods, with the use to which the good is put being the matter of moral concern. But justice is about distributing goods to people, and the central moral concern is with the benefits the goods will generate for the people. So his version of the excellence objection fails.

I share Cooper's view that one of the central values of education is in transmitting and fostering understanding knowledge and critical appreciation (though not for their own sake – for the sake of the good they do for those who receive them). Though nothing hinges on this, however, I would question his observation that concern with excellence implies concern only with scaling the heights. It seems plausible, for example, that English cheddar cheese is more excellent than American, even though the very best cheddar cheese is produced in Vermont, because the very best Vermont cheddar is only marginally better than the best English cheddar, and the remaining American cheddar is dreadful.

But nothing hinges on this, because no distributive conclusion can be reached merely from Cooper's observations even if they are true. When the state involves itself in distributing these goods it must bear in mind its obligation to treat its citizens equally. The argument I have made shows that, when the economy is structured to give unequal rewards, the principle that distributive outcomes should be deserved requires educational equality, even if that is to the detriment of some free-floating excellences. Given the importance of what is distributed by the economy for people's lives (money) and given the equal standing of citizens, the lover of educational excellence cannot just point out the relatively uncontroversial value of educational excellence: he must make an argument that this value is so important that its pursuit justifies distributing education so that those who cannot achieve excellence must also be further disadvantaged with respect to more readily accessible goods: those that money can buy.

Of course, the argument for educational equality assumes that labour market rewards are unequal. A strict egalitarian about the economy is on much stronger ground when advocating educational inequality for the purpose of excellence. But it is striking how rarely educational inegalitarians are material egalitarians.

● The second version of the excellence objection, that more able children deserve a superior education, is, while popular, absurd. We usually think that someone deserves a benefit only if they are responsible for some feature or action of themselves in virtue of which they deserve it. But no child is responsible for being more or less talented than other children; or for having been raised in an environment which supports their academic achievement. The desert version of the excellence objection, like the 'excellence in itself' version, would be less obnoxious if the children involved faced a labour market which did not offer unequal rewards to unequal levels of educational achievement, although it would still be problematic. But people who make this objection know only too well that children do face such labour markets.

● The most persuasive version of the excellence objection is the last: that we need to foster educational excellence in a few for the benefit of all members of society. High achievers become doctors, scientists, inventors, discoverers: people whose professional lives are spent producing benefits that the whole of society shares in. So those who are not able to achieve excellence have a powerful material interest in ensuring that those who can, do.

This argument is, of course, firmly in the egalitarian tradition: egalitarians generally do not claim that inequalities can never be justified, only that in order to be legitimate they must be justifiable in terms of the interests of the least well off.[29] Notice, too, that the objection, even if it does justify some selection, should lead to suspicion of any method of selection in which the background wealth or education level of parents threatens to be a factor in selection: as with the desert version of the excellence objection, proponents of this version should object to private schooling and to the mechanism which allows savvy parents to influence which schools their children will attend.

I am sure that the objection supports some public funding of selective higher education, so that people who are 18 and over who choose to take up socially valuable professions such as medicine and teaching are subsidized in their pursuit of the expensive training, provided that they use that training actually to pursue that profession. However, it is not clear to me how much selectivity it permits in primary and secondary education. I suspect that concession I have already made of not requiring that more resources be expended on the education of less able than on that of more able students probably suffices to neutralize this objection.

Because it is so pervasive in public debate I would like to make a final comment about the excellence objection in all its forms. One of the most troubling aspects of the objection is that those who make it rarely specify for whom they seek excellence. Cooper is fairly frank: he just wants the most able to be able to achieve the highest level of excellence compatible with everyone else being able to achieve some minimal threshold. But I, perhaps still infected by the democratic élan of the Enlightenment, feel unable to be so glib. To care about educational excellence without being concerned with every child's achievement of it seems to deny the equal concern and respect for individual persons that is the bedrock of the liberal state.

Consider the following, highly stylised table, in which different hypothetical systems are compared.

	System one	System two	System three	System four
Tony	165	130	90	105
Sid	75	110	90	108
Hattie	90	118	90	110
Total:	**330**	**358**	**270**	**323**

Does excellence require choosing the system with the highest individual level of achievement? System one surely cannot be superior to system two, which has a lower level of highest individual achievement, but higher levels of both equality and overall achievement. Could it require choosing the highest level of overall achievement? This again seems wrong: for this criterion makes system one superior to system four: yet system one gives us a massive level of inequality in return for a tiny gain in overall achievement.

There is a third thing that excellence advocacy could mean: it could mean that when we have a choice between strict equality and an unequal distribution in which all achieve at a higher level than any does in the system that yields equality, then, in our comparison, we should favour systems two and four to system three. This position seems to be correct, and it is correct because equality, though desirable, is not the only thing that is desirable. Individuals have reason to care about their relative position, but they also have reason to care about their absolute position. To seek to be worse off in any respect simply in order to be equally well off with others, who are also thereby made worse off, is not clearly rational.

Of course, the stylised example I have described does not exhaust the possibilities: policy-makers may be faced with other, harder, choices; and it will never be as clear to them as it is in my example what the effects of their policies will be on the distribution of excellence. But my figures were chosen not to help guide the policymaker, but to make the point that the excellence objection, even if it is accepted as permitting selection, needs a good deal more precision if it is to guide policy. When that precision is given, the objection either looks implausible, because it has no distributive constraint built into it, or looks as if it does not clearly justify selection.

Of course, there is an alternative way of trying to justify selection using a concern with educational excellence which is sensitive to distribution. The studies of 'tracking' or selection that demonstrate its bad effects on lower achievers identify a clear mechanism by which this occurs: the lower achievers become marked as such, less is expected of them, fewer resources are devoted to them, etc. This is the fault not of selection itself, but of the way selection has been pursued. Instead we could have academically selective schools in which the less able students attend schools where they have more resources, smaller classes, and greater attention devoted to them than do the academically more able. This is selective schooling with a twist: rather than identifying the advantaged children for special attention, we are identifying the disadvantaged for special attention, so that we can more efficiently raise their levels of achievement.

I see no principled reasons for rejecting this system. It violates the comprehensive ideal, but I believe that the principle of educational equality is far more important. But the system is not on the political agenda, and there are, furthermore, powerful reasons for thinking that it would not be politically sustainable. Parents whose children are identified as 'more able' at age 11 or 12 are liable to have access to coalition-building resources which they can direct to increasing the public resources devoted to the schools their children attend. The additional resources that must be directed to schools for those identified as less able will always be politically vulnerable when more and less able children are taught in separate schools. It is, of course, possible for better-resourced parents to lobby on behalf of their own children in common schools, but it is harder for them to monitor where the resources are going, and in general the extra resources needed for the less able are less vulnerable.

5
Conclusion

So educational equality is a fundamental value of social justice; it implies that inequalities of household income and wealth must be combated, and that the kinds of selection which continue to be deployed in the UK schooling system should be reformed in the ways I have suggested, and that the private sector is an enemy of social justice. A central fear of egalitarian reformers of the education system is that any egalitarian reforms will lead wealthier parents to opt out of the system into private schools. This is a reasonable fear, and it shows why any reform of the state system must be accompanied be reforms which simultaneously diminish the attractions of the private sector. But surely another cause of defections from the system is the constant stream of criticism directed at schools and teachers by newspapers and politicians, which gives understandably concerned parents an inaccurate impression of what the state system is doing. A government committed to egalitarian reform of the state school system should do what I have recommended: but it might start by being a little more economical with its criticisms of the system it runs and the people who try so hard to make it work.

Notes and References

[1]   I am grateful to Dan Hausman for extensive comments on earlier versions of this pamphlet, and for suggesting the topic. Thanks also to the editors of the series for extensive and valuable criticisms on the penultimate draft: John White also provided research help and a great deal of encouragement. Thanks also to Tim Brighouse for rapid response to factual questions, and to Lynn Glueck for everything.

[2]   Nick Davies, 'Political Coup Bred Educational Disaster', *The Guardian,* Sept. 16th 1999.

[3]   Nick Davies, 'Bias that killed the dream of equality', *The Guardian,* Sept. 15th 1999.

[4]   I have written extensively about the latter aim in 'Civic Education and Liberal Legitimacy', *Ethics* (1998) and *School Choice and Social Justice* (Oxford University Press, 2000) chapters 4 and 5.

[5]   I focus on economic circumstances here because, although crude, they are a proxy for many other features of a child's environment that affect her prospects. Of course, others may include race, education level of parents, and geographical location. Cultural background and the quality of parenting might be considered circumstances, or the choices of parents, depending on one's background view of these phenomena. I use the crude proxy to facilitate convenient exposition.

[6]   See Robert Nozick, *Anarchy, State and Utopia* (New York: Basic Books, 1974) and John Rawls, *A Theory of Justice* (Cambridge, Mass.: Harvard University Press, 1971). For the most searing refutation of Nozick see G.A. Cohen, *Self-Ownership Freedom and Equality* (Cambridge: Cambridge University Press, 1995) chapters 1 and 6.

[7]   It is worth mentioning that some critics of the principle of fair equality of opportunity advanced by John Rawls and related principles advocated by other theorist deny that we are properly held responsible for our exertion of effort, because inclination to exert effort is itself affected by factors for which we cannot be held responsible. See Richard Arneson, 'Against Rawlsian Equality of Opportunity', *Philosophical Studies* (1999).

[8]   Gewirtz, Ball and Bowe, *Markets, Choice and Equity in Education* (Buckingham: Open University Press, 1995). For a more comprehensive discussion of the effects on equality of choice schemes in general see Geoff Whitty et. al., *Devolution and Choice in Education* (Buckingham: Open University Press: 1998) especially pp. 115-125.

[9]   This is not to fault the design of the Gewirtz et. al. study – the researchers' interests were not exactly the same as mine, and they used the most feasible methods suited to their purposes.

[10]   Gewirtz et. al., *Markets, Choice and Equity in Education,* p 32.

[11]   Ibid., p. 44.

[12]   Ibid., p. 45.

[13]   Ibid., p. 47.

[14]   Ibid., pp. 141-2.

[15]   Ibid., p. 167.

[16]   Ibid., p. 167.

[17]   Ibid., at pp. 9-10.

[18]   Erik Olin Wright, 'Preface: The Real Utopias Project', in John Roemer et. al. *Equal Shares* (Verso: London, 1996), p. ix.

[19]   Means-testing is, in general, an undesirable mechanism. Means-tested benefits can create perverse incentives for adults who receive them (since when they reach the threshold of income at which the benefit disappears they face extraordinarily high marginal effective tax rates), and are furthermore vulnerable to opposition by powerful political coalitions (comprised of wealthier people who do not receive the benefit). But means-tested benefits which go directly to children seem quite politically robust (the Head Start program in the US, which gives pre-elementary schooling to poor children, is unique among US means-tested benefits in that it enjoys almost universal and still steadily increasing support among legislators).

[20]   *The Economist,* 3rd Feb 1996, 'Selective Schools: Britain's Labour Party is Wrong to Oppose them'.

21   James Tooley defends markets in education by pointing out, rightly, that the failure of the post 1988 settlement to deliver the goods reflects not on markets in schools, but on the structure of the particular imperfect market created by that settlement. But it is wrong to conclude, as he does, that perfect markets would do better. Perfect markets in schools are impossible for the reason I've given. This imperfection can be mitigated by the measure I'm proposing, but it can never be entirely removed. See James Tooley, *Education Without the State* (London: Institute for Economic Affairs, 1996).

22   Herbert Gintis, in 'The Political Economy of School Choice', *Teachers College Record*, (1995), canvasses the possibility of achieving equality in a selective system. He argues that the effects of selection in a thoroughly overhauled school system are uncertain, and that selective schools might be able to provide equal effective resources if more resources were spent in the schools with the less academically-able pupils. This seems quite possible to me, but I am assuming that my proposals would be adopted without a massive overhaul of the system, and that there would be serious political barriers to the differential funding required.

23   'The boy who scored a goal for inclusion', *Times Education Supplement,* August 6, 1999, p.5.

24   These ruminations were prompted by reading Steve Whitton's paper, 'Tracking and Educational Equality' (unpublished, on file with author) The stylized table discussed below is a modification of his own example.

25   John Wilson, 'Does Equality (of opportunity) make sense in education?' *Journal of Philosophy of Education*, 1991, p. 29.

26   David Cooper, *Illusions of Equality* (London: Routledge and Kegan Paul 1980) p. 54.

27   Cooper, p. 55.

28   Cooper, p. 57.

29   See John Rawls, *A Theory of Justice* (Cambridge, Mass.: Harvard University Press, 1971) for the *locus classicus* of this position.

Suggestions for further reading

Part One of this pamphlet develops an argument I have made in *School Choice and Social Justice*, chapter 6. In fact, the pamphlet version is an improvement on the book version, but there is, in the book, a much more elaborate discussion of alternative versions of educational equality.

Although I have tried to make my arguments accessible to readers with no background in philosophy, it is difficult to understand the preoccupations of political philosophers without some background reading. John Rawls's *A Theory of Justice* (op. cit) sets the stage for most contemporary anglophone political philosophy. The best introduction to Rawls is in Will Kymlicka *Contemporary Political Philosophy* (Clarendon Press: Oxford, 1990), chapter 2;and an unjustly neglected application of Rawls's theory to education can be found in Thomas Pogge, *Realizing Rawls* (Cornell University Press: Ithaca, 1989). For a brilliant critique of Rawls's principle of equality of opportunity see Richard Arneson, 'Against Rawlsian Equality of Opportunity', *Philosophical Studies* (1999).

Alternative conceptions of educational equality can be found in Randall Curren, 'Justice and the Threshold of Educational Equality', *Philosophy of Education,* (1995) and Amy Gutmann, *Democratic Education* (Princeton University Press: Princeton, 1987).

For objections to educational equality see David Cooper, *Illusions of Equality* (op. cit.) chapters 1-3, and John Wilson 'Does equality (of opportunity) in education makes sense?', *Journal of Philosophy of Education* ,1991. See also James Tooley, *Education Without the State* (op. cit.). I respond to some of these arguments in more detail in *School Choice and Social Justice,* chapter 7. In chapter 9 I elaborate and defend a school choice proposal that would implement educational equality.

New IMPACT Titles

IMPACT 4
March 2000

New Labour and the Future of Training

Christopher Winch
Professor of Philosophy of Education,
Nene-University College, Northampton

Within the framework of a discussion of the place of vocational aims among the aims of education in general, the pamphlet asks whether current post-16 training policy as put forward in the 1999 White Paper *Learning to Succeed* is likely to help deliver the government's stated target of a high skill economy.

There will be a symposium on IMPACT 4 at the Institute of Education on Tuesday afternoon, 14 March 2000. Among the respondents to Christopher Winch are:

Malcolm Wicks MP
Minister for Lifelong Learning

John Brennan
Association of Colleges

Frances O'Grady
TUC

For information please contact
Judy Morrison on 020 7612 6750, email j.morrison@ioe.ac.uk

Pamphlets can be ordered in advance at £5.99 plus £1 p. and p.
(£4.50 plus £1 for members of PESGB) from:

**The Education Bookshop, 20 Bedford Way, London WC1H OAL.
Tel: 0171-612-6050. Email: bmbc@ioe.ac.uk**

Topics of forthcoming titles from IMPACT

- Sex Education

- Personal, Social and Health Education

- Citizenship Education

- The National Curriculum after 2000

- The Place of Modern Foreign Languages in the Curriculum

- Good Teaching

- Gifted Pupils

- Environmental education

If you would like to be put on a mailing list for further information about the publication of these pamphlets and about any symposia or other events connected with their launch, please contact:

The Education Bookshop
20 Bedford Way, London WC1H 0AL
Telephone 020 7612 6050 Fax 020 7612 6407
Email: bmbc@ioe.ac.uk

BLACKWELL Journals

Journal of Philosophy of Education
The Journal of the Philosophy of Education Society of Great Britain

Edited by Richard Smith

The *Journal of Philosophy of Education* publishes articles representing a wide variety of philosophical traditions. They vary from examination of fundamental philosophical issues in their connection with education, to detailed critical engagement with current educational policy from a philosophical point of view. The journal aims to promote rigorous thinking on educational matters and to identify and criticise the ideological forces shaping education.

Recent and forthcoming highlights:
Political Liberalism and Civic Education, Stephen Mulhall
Paternalism and Consent, Haley Richmond
Rorty's Conception of Education, Eliyahu Rosenow
Europe and the World of Learning, Padraig Hogan
Teaching Mathematics, Yvette Solomon
Sex Education, David Archard

Special Issues:
Values, Virtues and Violence: Education and the Public Understanding of Morality (1999)
The Limits of Educational Assessment (1998)
Illusory Freedoms: Liberalism, Education and the Market (1997)
Quality and Education (1996)

Journal of Philosophy of Education ISSN 0309-8249 Published in March, July and November
Subscription Rates, Vol. 33/1999:
Institutions: Europe £224, N. America $413, Rest of World £250.
Personal: Europe £72, N. America $140, Rest of World £85.

To subscribe to Journal of Philosophy of Education please use the order form on the Blackwell website: http://www.blackwellpublishers.co.uk, send an email to jnlinfo@blackwellpublishers.co.uk, or contact either of the following:

- Blackwell Publishers Journals, PO Box 805, 108 Cowley Road, Oxford OX4 1FH, UK. Tel: +44 (0)1865 244083, fax +44 (0)1865 381381
- Journals Marketing (JOPE), Blackwell Publishers, 350 Main Street, Malden, MA 02148, USA. Tel. +1 (781) 388 8200, fax +1 (781) 388 8210

BLACKWELL *Publishers*

http://www.blackwellpublishers.co.uk

OXFORD

UNIVERSITY PRESS

School Choice and Social Justice
Professor Harry Brighouse

School choice, the leading educational reform proposal in the English-speaking world today, evokes extreme responses – its defenders present it as the saviour; its opponents as the deathnell of a fair educational system. Disagreement and vagueness about what constitutes social justice in education muddies the debate. The author provides a new theory of justice for education, arguing that justice requires that all children have a real opportunity to become autonomous persons, and that the state use a criterion of educational equality for deploying educational resources.
0-19-829586-3, 240 pp, HB
March 2000 £19.99

The Demands of Liberal Education
Meira Levinson

What should the aims of education be in a liberal society? Who should exercise control over children's education in a liberal state, and what form should the control take? How can children be taught to become good citizens of a pluralist state? *The Demands of Liberal Education* seeks to answer questions such as these by drawing upon political theory, philosophy of education, and empirical research to develop a liberal theory of children's education that is provocative and new.
0-19-829544-8, 250 pp, HB
August 1999 £20.00

NEW IN PAPERBACK
Creating Citizens
Political Education and Liberal Democracy

In lucid and elegant prose, Professor Callan, one of the world's foremost philosophers of education, identifies both the principal ends of civic education, and the rights that limit their political pursuit.
0-19-829647-9, 280 pp
November 1999 £15.99

For further information on Politics books from Oxford, visit our website
www.oup.co.uk

Discover new book by e-mail
www.oup.co.uk/emailnews

24-hr credit hotline
+44 (0)1536 454534

Ref: 10HSIPE99

Join the

Philosophy of Education Society of Great Britain
and receive the
Journal of Philosophy of Education

FREE!

Formed in 1964, the Society exists to promote the study, teaching and application of Philosophy of Education. It holds an annual three-day conference as well as local branch meetings and conferences. Members receive the *Journal of Philosophy of Education* as part of the benefits of their annual membership.

Membership rates:

(worldwide) £24.00 (£12.00 unwaged; £8.00 non-Western income as determined by the Executive Committee). Payment by credit card possible (with £2.00 surcharge).

Membership enquiries: please contact

Dr Colin Wringe,
Department of Education
University of Keele
Staffordshire ST5 5BG UK

E-mail: eda26@cc.keele.ac.uk